## THIS COUPON ENTITLES YOU TO

# ONE BLINDFOLD **BLOWJOB**

Wear a blindfold while I pleasure your throbbing manhood
with my mouth, lips, tongue and breath

## THIS COUPON ENTITLES YOU TO

# HEAVY **PETTING**

20 minute hot foreplay session in a location of your choice
(restrain from having full sex to intensify the sexual tension)

I want to get

# HOT & HEAVY

with you

---

I want to get

# HOT & HEAVY

with you

# ONE LICK **IT OFF SESSION**

I'll cover your body with something sweet and sticky then slowly lick it off

# FULL **BODY MASSAGE**

45 minute intimate massage covering EVERY inch of your hot body

I want to get

# HOT & HEAVY

with you

---

I want to get

# HOT & HEAVY

with you

## THIS COUPON ENTITLES YOU TO

# SEXUAL **FANTASY PLAY**

One of your wettest, dirtiest dreams brought to life

## THIS COUPON ENTITLES YOU TO

# PRICK **TEASE**

20 minute private lap dance finishing with a full striptease
(no touching the dancer during the act please)

I want to get

# HOT & HEAVY

with you

---

I want to get

# HOT & HEAVY

with you

## THIS COUPON ENTITLES YOU TO

# A KITCHEN **QUICKIE**

Against the sink, over the counter, on top of the washing machine - you decide
(must not last longer than six minutes and must be fully clothed - side pantie style)

## THIS COUPON ENTITLES YOU TO

# NO **HANDS**

Up to 20 minutes of caressing and teasing your body with my lips, tongue,
breath, skin… anything EXCEPT my hands

I want to get

# HOT & HEAVY

with you

---

I want to get

# HOT & HEAVY

with you

# ONE HOTEL **HOOKUP**

Let's get dressed up and pretend we're strangers who meet at a bar then proceed to having a sordid one night stand in a cheap hotel

# FRUITY **LUBES**

Let's experiment with as many fruity flavored lubes as we can handle

I want to get

# HOT & HEAVY

with you

---

I want to get

# HOT & HEAVY

with you

# A SEX **MARATHON SESSION**

Sex all night long (or until we're too exhausted to continue)

# EROTIC **RE-ENACTMENT**

That hot scene from a sexy movie you've enjoyed... let's do it

I want to get

# HOT & HEAVY

with you

---

I want to get

# HOT & HEAVY

with you

# EXPERIMENTAL **PLAY**

Experiment with sex toys or food items of your choosing

# MORNING **SEX**

Midweek quickie before work, or slow and sleepy weekender - your choice

I want to get

# HOT & HEAVY

with you

---

I want to get

# HOT & HEAVY

with you

## THIS COUPON ENTITLES YOU TO

# NAKED **COOK**

I'll prepare your meal with nothing on except heels and a smile
(includes meal prep, cooking, consumption, clearing and dish washing)

## THIS COUPON ENTITLES YOU TO

# CUM **DUMP**

Free pass to 'finish' all over my face or any other part of my body

I want to get

# HOT & HEAVY

with you

---

I want to get

# HOT & HEAVY

with you

# WATCH **BUT DON'T TOUCH**

Watch as I pleasure myself until climax. You can pleasure yourself as you watch (no touching each other during the act. Post masturbation sex is permitted)

# SEX **SHOP**

Visit to the naughty shop! I'll let you pick an outfit or toy we can enjoy later

I want to get

# HOT & HEAVY

with you

- - - - - - - - - - - - - - - - - - - - - - - - - - - - - -

I want to get

# HOT & HEAVY

with you

# ONE **BONDAGE SESSION**

Someone is gong to be tied-up and f**ked tonight - you choose who
(the safe word is: _____ )

# ANAL **PLEASURE**

I'll let you play with my ass-hole. A finger, a tongue, a toy or something more

I want to get

# HOT & HEAVY

with you

---

I want to get

# HOT & HEAVY

with you

## THIS COUPON ENTITLES YOU TO

# PHONE **SEX**

I'll tell you all the dirty, smutty things I desperately want to do to you
(must not be in the same house or building at time of call)

## THIS COUPON ENTITLES YOU TO

# NO **PANTIES**

I'll go commando for the entire day
(spice things up further by combining with the Phone Sex coupon)

I want to get
# HOT & HEAVY
with you

---

I want to get
# HOT & HEAVY
with you

## THIS COUPON ENTITLES YOU TO

# A SEXY **GAMES NIGHT**

Think strip poker, naked Twister, dirty darts or something else

## THIS COUPON ENTITLES YOU TO

# STEAMY **SHOWER SEX**

Let's do it just like they do in the movies

I want to get

# HOT & HEAVY

with you

---

I want to get

# HOT & HEAVY

with you

## THIS COUPON ENTITLES YOU TO

# SEX **IN THE WILD**

Let's do it in the backyard, up against a tree, a secluded beach or elsewhere
(Disclaimer: keep it legal - any action you take is at your own risk)

## THIS COUPON ENTITLES YOU TO

# SENSUAL **LOVEMAKING**

Take it sloooow. Lots of touching, caressing, licking, panting and eye gazing

I want to get

# HOT & HEAVY

with you

---

I want to get

# HOT & HEAVY

with you

## THIS COUPON ENTITLES YOU TO

# DISCOVERY **SEX**

Share three sexy things you enjoy or would like to try, then we'll do them

## THIS COUPON ENTITLES YOU TO

# SEX **IN A TINY PLACE**

Like in the car, the closet or toilet

I want to get

# HOT & HEAVY

with you

---

I want to get

# HOT & HEAVY

with you

## THIS COUPON ENTITLES YOU TO

# EROTIC **STORY TIME**

Up to 60 minutes (if we can last that long) of reading erotica to each other

## THIS COUPON ENTITLES YOU TO

# ONE **INTIMACY WORKSHOP**

A tantric sex session, naked yoga, couples massage or something else

I want to get

# HOT & HEAVY

with you

---

I want to get

# HOT & HEAVY

with you

# PLAY **WITH ME ANYWAY**

Stroke my private parts while in a public place like an elevator or restaurant
(Be discreet, don't get caught - any action you take is at your own risk)

# CUDDLE-FREE **SEX**

Sometimes you want to roll over and fall asleep after the act - here you go

I want to get

# HOT & HEAVY

with you

---

I want to get

# HOT & HEAVY

with you

## WILDCARD COUPON

## WILDCARD COUPON

I want to get
# HOT & HEAVY
with you

---

I want to get
# HOT & HEAVY
with you

## WILDCARD COUPON

_____

## WILDCARD COUPON

_____

I want to get

# HOT & HEAVY

with you

---

I want to get

# HOT & HEAVY

with you

## WILDCARD COUPON

_____

## WILDCARD COUPON

_____

I want to get

# HOT & HEAVY

with you

---

I want to get

# HOT & HEAVY

with you

## WILDCARD COUPON

## WILDCARD COUPON

Printed in Great Britain
by Amazon

35441212R00024